PITCH NOTES

Pitch Notes

Soccer Journal

Richard Kent & Amy Edwards

A companion book to

*Writing on the Bus: Using Athletic Team Notebooks and Journals
to Advance Learning and Performance in Sports*

WritingAthletes.com

Dedications:

For Bill Morgan, teacher, coach, and friend... *RK*

For Alex Skotarek who coached me to the next level... *AE*

Acknowledgments:

Our thanks to Sheila Stawinski of the University of Vermont for her permission to modify and use her Performance Feedback form. Thanks to Gayle Sirois for her editorial eye.

This book is published in cooperation with the National Writing Project, University of California, 2105 Bancroft Way, Berkeley, CA 94720

CONTENTS

WRITING YOUR GAME

For you as a player, keeping a soccer journal is about learning and improving. Whether you're training at a soccer camp, practicing on your own, or starting a new season with your team, writing in this journal can help you progress as an athlete by thinking about and analyzing your play.

As we explained in the *Soccer Team Notebook*, just writing about your training and match play isn't going to replace good coaching or dedicated training. You're not going to instantaneously run faster or score more goals because you wrote a journal entry. But completing the activities in this journal will make you a more knowledgeable soccer player. With that knowledge you can improve. That's exactly why Olympians and other elite athletes write in training logs, journals, and team notebooks.

Before each section of this journal, you'll find instructions and in some cases a model. Here are the sections of your journal:

Soccer Journal Prompts: forty-eight (48) journal prompts to help you think about your game and yourself. If a particular prompt doesn't work for you, cross it out and write what's uppermost in your mind.

Additional Journal Pages: seven (7) extra pages when you have more to say about a particular journal prompt.

Match Analyses I: sixteen (16) analysis pages that will guide you in analyzing a match you played in. Even if you sat the bench, analyze the match! This experience is about learning and knowing the game.

Performance Feedback: five (5) pages that will help you think about the stressors you face before, during, and after a match.

Match Analyses II: three (3) analysis pages that will guide you in unpacking a match you watched in person, on video, or online.

Notes Pages: five (5) blank pages and six soccer field outlines to use for notes, set-piece drawings, team formations, and more.

We want to emphasize that this is your journal. Write what's true for you as a player and person. Address your weaknesses—don't avoid them—and focus on improvement.

We challenge you to think deeply, to explore your understanding of soccer, and to see yourself at the next level of *the beautiful game*. Visualize your best—then plan and practice to get there.

SOCCER JOURNAL PROMPTS

Instructions for Writing Journals

Your journal includes 48 prompts. Many of these prompts can be composed in 3-5 minutes; they're called Quick Write Journals. When you begin a journal entry, try not to stop; keep your pen or pencil on the paper and keep writing. Quick writes remind us of one-touch drills that we use in practice: our players must be inventive and keep moving!

If your mind goes blank while you're writing a journal entry, make a list of words related to the topic. When your ideas begin to flow, start writing sentences again. If you run out of space and have more to say, continue writing on the additional blank journal pages provided on pages 59-66. And please don't be overly concerned about the conventions of writing like spelling, grammar, or paragraphing. Just write.

1.

What are your strengths as a soccer player right now? When asked to name
a strength, some players said that they were …

Focused	Dedicated	Fit	Inventive
Confident	Competitive	Motivated	Brave
Responsible	Positive	Skillful	Strong

List some of your strengths here:

Now write about your primary strength as a player…

2.

Think about an aspect of soccer that you'd like to improve upon. Maybe you'd like to be a better shooter or create more innovative corner kicks. Search YouTube or other Websites to find a video on shooting or corner kick set-ups. Watch the video and write about what you observed:

Skill: _________________ Title of Video: _________________________________

—What new information did you learn?

—What might you try out or how might you adapt your play?

—What questions did you have after watching the video?

—What ideas might you share with a fellow player?

—What knowledge might you share with your coach?

—What suggestions might you make for revising this video:

3.

Mental Imagery: Think back and recall your best moments as a player. Remember the exact details of a perfect pass, brilliant move, or powerful run. Make a list of those moments and create your own mental performance video that you can play back to yourself in preparation for a game, or to use during a competition to gain back confidence. Your mental performance video might last between 10-30 seconds.

Image:

Image:

Image:

Image:

Image:

4.

Write about one of your favorite teammates, training partners, or opponents.

Name or initials: _______________________

Qualities as an athlete:

Qualities as a person:

Unique habits or quirks:

A story you'd share about this athlete:

What have you learned from this athlete?

More:

5.

Write about your strengths and/or challenges with the following:

Dribbling:

Heading:

Juggling:

Shooting:

Shooting laces:

Chip pass:

Shielding the ball:

Tackling:

Throw-in:

Corner Kicks:

Penalty Kicks:

Chest Trap:

Of these 12 skills which two do you really need to work on? Explain:

6.

Who brings out the best in you as a soccer player and why? You might first think of a coach, manager, or trainer. But also think about family members, friends, fans, teammates, or even an opponent.

7.

What makes training hard for you?

What makes training easy for you?

8.

My favorite training food is . . .

During a soccer match I am nervous about . . .

My favorite exercise or activity during a training session is . . .

When I hear _______________________________ from an opponent or an opponent's fan, I feel like . . .

When my team wins a match by a wide margin, I . . .

When my coach says __________________________ I feel like . . .

9.

Make a list of your favorite "things" in soccer. They could be plays, equipment, moments, places, or people. Here's an example: the 30 seconds after a sudden death, overtime win.

10.

Outline what you consider a perfect warm-up routine for a training session. Make a list of each activity on the left; then include the approximate amount of time spent on the activity and offer a reason you have included it.

Warm-up Activities   How long?   Why this activity?

11.

Write a letter to one of your former coaches. You may wish to include: what you're doing now as a player; the coach's contributions to your life; the issues you currently face as a player; a fun memory; a photo. You may wish to mail a revised version of the letter to your former coach.

12.

"Some days, playing poorly is the most important result that could happen." Give an example from your own experience as an athlete why this statement can be true.

13.

How do you learn soccer? Look at this figure and circle the ways you learn as a player.

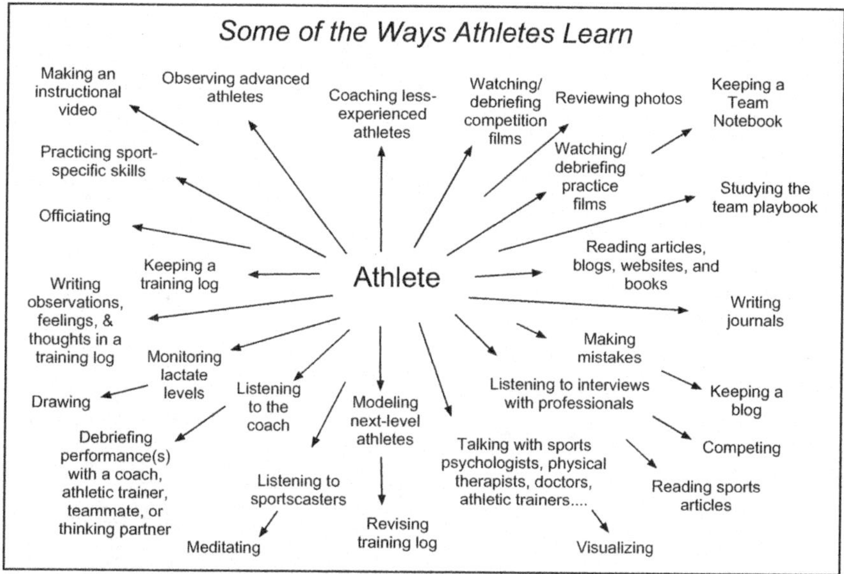

Reprinted with permission, *Writing on the Bus (Kent, 2012, p. 14)*

From the various learning activities above that you did <u>not</u> circle, which ones could you add to your experience to help you improve as a player? Explain.

Are there ways you learn that are not included in the figure above?

14.

Describe your most humiliating experience as an athlete. What might you have learned from this experience?

15.

In this journal entry, you're going to create a soccer playlist.

Make a list of your favorite songs down the left side:

Which favorite songs would you play…

The night before an important match:

Song title: _______________________

During training:

Song title: _______________________

The morning of a match:

Song title: _______________________

During a match:

Song title: _______________________

After an upset win:

Song title: _______________________

After a loss to an opponent you could have beaten:

Song title: _______________________

When the season ends:

Song title: _______________________

Others times: _______________________

Song title: _______________________

Others times: _______________________

Song title: _______________________

16.

Using your most recent competition, respond to the following:

—Describe the evening before this competition. Did you prepare the way you should have?

—On game day, how did you spend your time? Did you eat/hydrate adequately? If you could improve one aspect of your preparation for this competition, what would it be?

—Describe your pre-game preparation (e.g., warm-up). Is there any aspect of your pre-game that you'd improve upon?

—Describe your mindset <u>during</u> the competition. Were you focused and motivated?

—Describe your post-game recovery. Did you stretch, hydrate, and eat appropriately? Is there any aspect of your post-game that you'd change?

17.

Describe your earliest memories as a soccer player.

18.

Make a list of five qualities you believe an effective coach must have. Give an example from a coach you know.

Quality ___________________________________:

Quality ___________________________________:

Quality ___________________________________:

Quality ___________________________________:

Quality ___________________________________:

19.

Think about the role of soccer coaches and officials. Maybe you've done some coaching or officiating in soccer. Maybe not. Whatever your experience, write about the following prompts:

–What are the most challenging aspects of being a soccer coach?

–What are some of the most challenging aspects of being a soccer official?

–As a player, is there anything you could do to assist coaches or officials with their jobs?

20.

Describe the last time you lost your cool in a match. How did it affect your play? Did anyone say anything to you? What did you learn from this experience?

21.

If you could relive one moment as a soccer player, what would it be and why would you want to go back?

22.

Picture a younger athlete who might admire you. How would that player describe you as an athlete and a person?

23.

Write from the perspective of your youngest competitive self about the athlete you have become. Begin with this opening:

Dear _________________,

When I was ____ *years old, I dreamed about being an older athlete like you are now. I thought that I would be ...*

Now, I am ...

24.

What is something you dislike about yourself as an athlete? Write about how you confront or work on this issue in an effort to improve.

25.

Think back through your athletic career and make a list of the teams you've played on or the age levels you competed at. What did you learn at each level? Who do you remember from those days? You can also include experiences like pick-up games at your local pitch.

Team/Age Group________________________:

Team/Age Group________________________:

Team/Age Group________________________:

Team/Age Group________________________:

Team/Age Group________________________:

Team/Age Group________________________:

Team/Age Group________________________:

26.

In soccer, there are things we can control and things we can't. For example, we can't control the weather, our coach's decisions, or what someone says about us. We can control the amount of sleep we get, the volume and quality of training we do, the diet we maintain, and the attitude we bring to a practice or match. Write about a time when you let something you could <u>not</u> control get the better of you. What happened? How did you react? What would you do now under the same circumstances?

27.

How do you prepare for a game? Many players have routines that they follow. They may go to bed at a certain time, eat specific foods, listen to particular music, or talk with certain people. Some players review their own "game plans" and, using mental imagery, "watch" their mental performance video like you created in Journal #3 on page 13. Write about your pre-match routines. If you have not established one or wish to revise the one you have, write about that.

28.

Make a list of five good things that are happening in your life right now outside of sport. Select one or two and write about them.

1. ____

2. ____

3. ____

4. ____

5. ____

29.

It's often said that we are who we spend the most time with. Who are the five people, athletes or not, that you spend the most time with? In what ways do they influence who you are?

30.

Make a list of what you say to yourself during a soccer game. You may well want to write down this "self-talk" just after a game or competition. This internal dialog may include feelings ("We're going to destroy this team."), instructions you give yourself ("Hang back! Delay! Wait until she makes her move."), or random thoughts ("What did that fan just say to Alex?")

31.

Read through your list of self-talk on the previous page and write about what you notice. Is your talk positive, instructive, and motivating? Do you spend too much time complaining about a teammate, the coach, or an official? In the end, you'll want to decide whether your talk is productive or destructive, positive or negative, informative or unhelpful.

32.

Make a list of 10 favorite quotations by soccer players or athletes. You may find lists of quotations by athletes by searching the Internet.

33.

What's the best soccer match or other competition that you've seen in person? Describe the details and explain what made it *the best*.

34.

Make a list of people—athletes or not—that you would stand in a very long line to meet. What do these people have in common? In your eyes, what does this list say about you?

35.

What is your favorite place to compete and why?

———

36.

Throughout your time as a player, you may have discovered some favorite resources that you've used to expand your knowledge and enjoyment of soccer. Make a list of the Websites, YouTube videos, books, magazines, Facebook pages, or movies that you would recommend to a younger soccer player. If you don't have many, ask friends or teammates for their favorites.

37.

What is a good opponent?

38.

Watch a match on television, online, or a video. Make a list of some the announcer's best descriptive lines. What's your favorite and why?

39.

Under each category below, name a teammate, soccer camp friend, or even an opponent. Give an example or two of the athlete's qualities.

Tag a Teammate

Who'd make a great coach?	A true sportsman	Dedication plus	Kindest
Most coachable	Always leaves it on the field	Most motivating	Great future
Great opponent	Team Leader	Fun	Positive
Healthy	Student-Athlete: the complete package	Who should take the last shot	Fitness Fanatic

40.

A class of sports psychology students explored how failure can be helpful. Among the list compiled by students were the following—write about them:

Failure found what didn't work.

Failure adds value to success.

Failure creates hunger to do better.

Failure is feedback.

41.

What advice or talk do you <u>least</u> like to hear before an important game? Why?

42.

Come up with four t-shirt slogans/sayings about your team, soccer, competing, or training. Use the t-shirts provided. To jumpstart your thinking, here is the Republic of Ireland's slogan for UEFA Euro 2012:

Talk with your feet. Play with your heart.

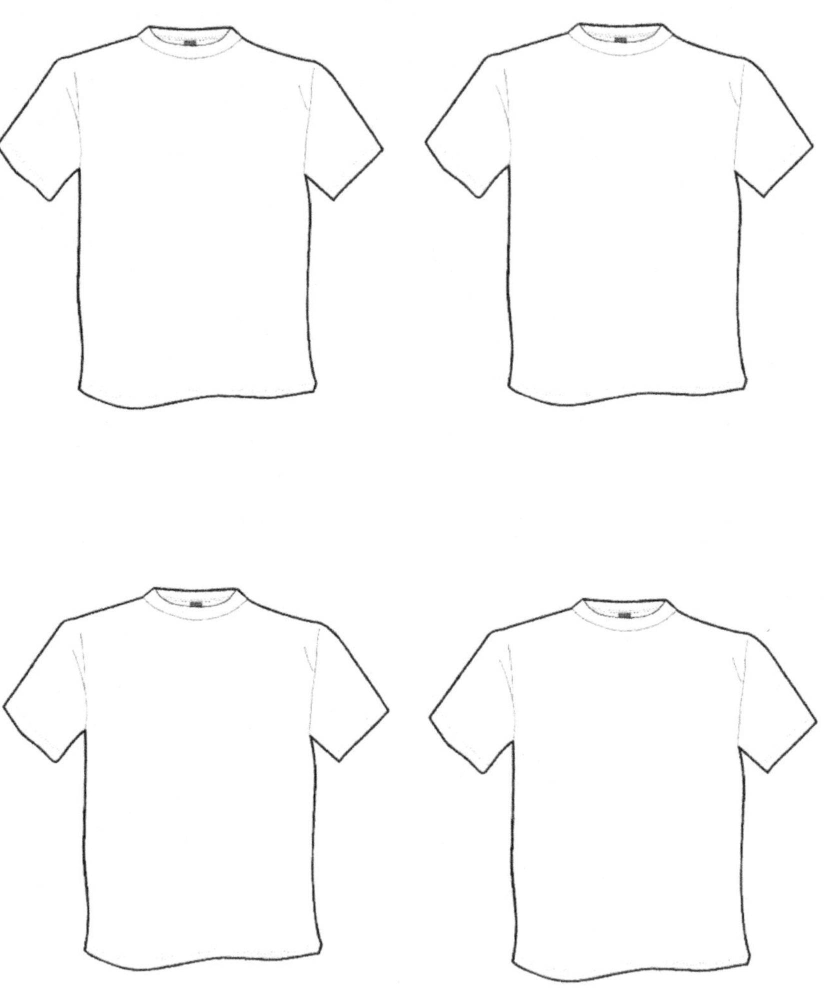

43.

"Somewhere behind the athlete you've become and the hours of practice and the coaches who have pushed you is a little girl who fell in love with the game and never looked back... play for her."

Write about this quotation from soccer legend Mia Hamm.

44.

Draw a picture of your favorite piece of sports equipment and write one sentence about it.

45.

Write about the kindest thing you have ever done as an athlete.

55

46.

Throughout a soccer season, tour, or camp, you experience highs and lows, ups and down. Think back and give quick examples of the following:

I laughed…

I cried or got emotional…

I screamed like a wild person…

I got crazy angry…

I sat and stared in disbelief…

I just didn't care…

I wanted to go hide…

I wanted someone to see…

47.

We are our thoughts and actions. In the callout bubble below, list the <u>individual</u> words (not phrases or sentences) that you believe represent you as both an athlete and person.

48.

"Writing organizes and clarifies our thoughts. Writing is how we think our way into a subject and make it our own. Writing enables us to find out what we know—and what we don't know—about whatever we're trying to learn." –William Zinsser

In what ways has this quotation proven true for you as an athlete who has kept a journal?

ADDITIONAL JOURNAL PAGES

Journal #______

Journal #______

Journal #______

Journal #______

Journal #______

Journal #_______

Journal #______

MATCH ANALYSIS I

Instructions for *Match Analysis I*

The prompts on these pages provide you with an opportunity to analyze your match. Unpacking a soccer game in this fashion, whether you were a reserve or played every minute, helps you think more objectively while seeing the larger picture of a game. This thinking will help you improve your understanding of soccer. The *MAI* may be used for scrimmages, *friendlies*, and even intrasquad contests as well as your league or conference matches.

When you fill out an *MAI*, don't be overly concerned about the conventions of writing. In other words, don't worry about spelling, grammar, and paragraphing... *just write*.

Check out the model *MAI* on the next page and look closely at the way the player addressed certain prompts. But remember, these are just models—you'll have your own way of telling the story of a match.

In the final section of the *MAI*, you'll see a Player Check-in. This section can usually be accomplished quickly. Don't sit around and ponder life. Give a general response that reflects your immediate thought. Rate each topic in the Player Check-in using the following scale:

Above Average (+)　　　　Average (O)　　　　Below Average (–)

As you go through these topics, focus on the following:

Health:　　　　How's my over all health?

Sleep:　　　　Am I getting enough sleep each night?

Hydration:　　　　Do I take in enough water throughout the day as well as before, during, and after a match?

Fitness:　　　　How's my overall fitness level?

Nutrition:　　　　The USDA has a basic informational Website that offers nutritional guidance about the consumption of food (see ChooseMyPlate.Gov). For purposes of the Player Check-in, ask yourself whether you've eaten the suggested foods of a healthy diet (i.e., grains, proteins, veggies, fruit).

—MODEL—

Match Analysis I

Opponent: *Leavitt (W 3 L 1 D 0)* Date: *9/18* Result: *1-0 W* Pitch: *Home*
Record: Wins: 4 Losses: 0 Draws: 0   Minutes Played: 88 minutes

- My strengths as a player in today's match:
Maintained defense's compactness. Right amount of talk—I didn't talk too much like at Lisbon. I had a <u>brilliant</u> run into the attacking third… ☺

- My weaknesses as a player in today's match:
I could have been more supportive of Jason. When I encourage him he plays better.

- Team strengths in today's match:
We worked as a team—great support—positive comments… Good halftime adjustments.

- Team weaknesses in today's match:
We could have been more inventive in attack during the 2nd half. We used Matt too much.

- Opponent's strengths:
LHS never let down. #9 had warp-speed. His runs opened space and chances on goal.

- Opponent's weaknesses:
Their midfielders and forwards did not mark us well in attack.

- What was the "difference" in today's match:
Our midfielders' support of the forwards…and, did I mention, a brilliant run by the sweeper?

- What team adjustment would you suggest for the next match against this opponent?

  #9=FAST. Move Dusty? More variety in attack.

- Who was the Player of the Match and why?
Ryan's save in the second half kept the match at 1-0. He came out bravely, as you would say, and took the ball off the offender's foot.

- Other comments (e.g., team strategy, attitude, preparation….)

  We were prepared! The seniors had us ready to play. Un-DE-feated!

Player Check-in

Above Average (+)   Average (O)   Below Average (–)

Health	+	*Nutrition:*	Grains	O
Sleep	O		Protein	+
Hydration	O		Veggies	–
Fitness	+		Fruit	O

Life Beyond Soccer O

Quotable Quote:

The guy's not human!" by Dusty about #9 LHS

Match Analysis I

Opponent: ______________ (W __ L __ D__) *Date:* _______ Result: ____
Pitch: ____________Our Record: Wins: ___ Losses: ____ Draws: ___
Minutes Played: _____

- My strengths as a player in today's match:

- My weaknesses as a player in today's match:

- Team strengths in today's match:

- Team weaknesses in today's match:

- Opponent's strengths:

- Opponent's weaknesses:

- What was the "difference" in today's match:

- What team adjustment would you suggest for the next match against this opponent?

- Who was the Player of the Match and why?

- Other comments (e.g., team strategy, attitude, preparation....)

Player Check-in

Above Average (+)   Average (O)   Below Average (–)

Health ___	*Nutrition:*	Grains ___
Sleep ___		Protein ___
Hydration ___		Veggies ___
Fitness ___		Fruit ___

Life Beyond Soccer ___

Quotable Quote:

____

____

Match Analysis I

Opponent: ______________ (W __ L __ D__) *Date:* _______ Result: ____
Pitch: ____________ Our Record: Wins: ___ Losses: ____ Draws: ___
Minutes Played: _____

- My strengths as a player in today's match:

- My weaknesses as a player in today's match:

- Team strengths in today's match:

- Team weaknesses in today's match:

- Opponent's strengths:

- Opponent's weaknesses:

–   What was the "difference" in today's match:

–   What team adjustment would you suggest for the next match against this opponent?

–   Who was the Player of the Match and why?

–   Other comments (e.g., team strategy, attitude, preparation….)

Player Check-in

Above Average (+)   Average (O)   Below Average (–)

Health	____	*Nutrition:*	Grains ____
Sleep	____		Protein ____
Hydration ____			Veggies ____
Fitness	____		Fruit ____

Life Beyond Soccer ____

Quotable Quote:

____

____

Match Analysis I

Opponent: _____________ (W __ L __ D__) *Date:* _______ Result: ___
Pitch: ____________Our Record: Wins: ___ Losses: ___ Draws: ___
Minutes Played: _____

- My strengths as a player in today's match:

- My weaknesses as a player in today's match:

- Team strengths in today's match:

- Team weaknesses in today's match:

- Opponent's strengths:

- Opponent's weaknesses:

- What was the "difference" in today's match:

- What team adjustment would you suggest for the next match against this opponent?

- Who was the Player of the Match and why?

- Other comments (e.g., team strategy, attitude, preparation....)

Player Check-in

Above Average (+)   Average (O)   Below Average (–)

Health	___	*Nutrition:*	Grains	___
Sleep	___		Protein	___
Hydration	___		Veggies	___
Fitness	___		Fruit	___

Life Beyond Soccer ___

Quotable Quote:

____

____

Match Analysis I

Opponent: _____________ (W __ L __ D__) *Date:* _______ Result: ___
Pitch: _____________Our Record: Wins: ___ Losses: ___ Draws: ___
Minutes Played: _____

-   My strengths as a player in today's match:

-   My weaknesses as a player in today's match:

-   Team strengths in today's match:

-   Team weaknesses in today's match:

-   Opponent's strengths:

-   Opponent's weaknesses:

–   What was the "difference" in today's match:

–   What team adjustment would you suggest for the next match against this opponent?

–   Who was the Player of the Match and why?

–   Other comments (e.g., team strategy, attitude, preparation….)

Player Check-in

Above Average (+)   Average (O)   Below Average (–)

Health ____	*Nutrition:*	Grains ____
Sleep ____		Protein ____
Hydration ____		Veggies ____
Fitness ____		Fruit ____

Life Beyond Soccer ____

Quotable Quote:

____

____

Match Analysis I

Opponent: _____________ (W __ L __ D__) *Date:* ______ Result: ___
Pitch: ____________Our Record: Wins: ___ Losses: ___ Draws: ___
Minutes Played: _____

- My strengths as a player in today's match:

- My weaknesses as a player in today's match:

- Team strengths in today's match:

- Team weaknesses in today's match:

- Opponent's strengths:

- Opponent's weaknesses:

- What was the "difference" in today's match:

- What team adjustment would you suggest for the next match against this opponent?

- Who was the Player of the Match and why?

- Other comments (e.g., team strategy, attitude, preparation….)

Player Check-in

Above Average (+)   Average (O)   Below Average (–)

Health	____	*Nutrition:*	Grains ____
Sleep	____		Protein ____
Hydration	____		Veggies ____
Fitness	____		Fruit ____

Life Beyond Soccer ____

Quotable Quote:

———————————————————————————

———————————————————————————

Match Analysis I

Opponent: ____________ (W __ L __ D__) *Date:* ______ Result: ___
Pitch: ___________Our Record: Wins: ___ Losses: ___ Draws: ___
Minutes Played: _____

- My strengths as a player in today's match:

- My weaknesses as a player in today's match:

- Team strengths in today's match:

- Team weaknesses in today's match:

- Opponent's strengths:

- Opponent's weaknesses:

- What was the "difference" in today's match:

- What team adjustment would you suggest for the next match against this opponent?

- Who was the Player of the Match and why?

- Other comments (e.g., team strategy, attitude, preparation….)

Player Check-in

Above Average (+)   Average (O)   Below Average (–)

Health	____	*Nutrition:*	Grains	____
Sleep	____		Protein	____
Hydration	____		Veggies	____
Fitness	____		Fruit	____

Life Beyond Soccer ____

Quotable Quote:

____

____

Match Analysis I

Opponent: ______________ (W __ L __ D__) *Date:* ______ Result: ___
Pitch: ____________Our Record: Wins: ___ Losses: ___ Draws: ___
Minutes Played: _____

- My strengths as a player in today's match:

- My weaknesses as a player in today's match:

- Team strengths in today's match:

- Team weaknesses in today's match:

- Opponent's strengths:

- Opponent's weaknesses:

– What was the "difference" in today's match:

– What team adjustment would you suggest for the next match against this opponent?

– Who was the Player of the Match and why?

– Other comments (e.g., team strategy, attitude, preparation....)

Player Check-in

Above Average (+)   Average (O)   Below Average (–)

Health	____	*Nutrition:*	Grains	____
Sleep	____		Protein	____
Hydration	____		Veggies	____
Fitness	____		Fruit	____

Life Beyond Soccer ____

Quotable Quote:

____

____

Match Analysis I

Opponent: _____________ (W __ L __ D__) *Date:* ______ Result: ___
Pitch: ____________Our Record: Wins: ___ Losses: ___ Draws: ___
Minutes Played: _____

- My strengths as a player in today's match:

- My weaknesses as a player in today's match:

- Team strengths in today's match:

- Team weaknesses in today's match:

- Opponent's strengths:

- Opponent's weaknesses:

- What was the "difference" in today's match:

- What team adjustment would you suggest for the next match against this opponent?

- Who was the Player of the Match and why?

- Other comments (e.g., team strategy, attitude, preparation....)

Player Check-in

Above Average (+)   Average (O)   Below Average (–)

Health ____	*Nutrition:*	Grains ____
Sleep ____		Protein ____
Hydration ____		Veggies ____
Fitness ____		Fruit ____

Life Beyond Soccer ____

Quotable Quote:

____

____

Match Analysis I

Opponent: ______________ (W __ L __ D__) *Date:* _______ Result: ____
Pitch: _____________Our Record: Wins: ____ Losses: ____ Draws: ____
Minutes Played: _____

- My strengths as a player in today's match:

- My weaknesses as a player in today's match:

- Team strengths in today's match:

- Team weaknesses in today's match:

- Opponent's strengths:

- Opponent's weaknesses:

– What was the "difference" in today's match:

– What team adjustment would you suggest for the next match against this opponent?

– Who was the Player of the Match and why?

– Other comments (e.g., team strategy, attitude, preparation....)

Player Check-in

Above Average (+)   Average (O)   Below Average (–)

Health	____	*Nutrition:*	Grains	____
Sleep	____		Protein	____
Hydration	____		Veggies	____
Fitness	____		Fruit	____

Life Beyond Soccer ____

Quotable Quote:

____

____

Match Analysis I

Opponent: ______________ (W __ L __ D__) *Date:* _______ Result: ____
Pitch: ____________Our Record: Wins: ___ Losses: ___ Draws: ___
Minutes Played: _____

- My strengths as a player in today's match:

- My weaknesses as a player in today's match:

- Team strengths in today's match:

- Team weaknesses in today's match:

- Opponent's strengths:

- Opponent's weaknesses:

–   What was the "difference" in today's match:

–   What team adjustment would you suggest for the next match against this opponent?

–   Who was the Player of the Match and why?

–   Other comments (e.g., team strategy, attitude, preparation….)

Player Check-in

Above Average (+)   Average (O)   Below Average (–)

Health	____	*Nutrition:* Grains	____
Sleep	____	Protein	____
Hydration	____	Veggies	____
Fitness	____	Fruit	____

Life Beyond Soccer ____

Quotable Quote:

____

____

Match Analysis I

Opponent: _____________ (W __ L __ D__) *Date:* _______ Result: ____
Pitch: ____________Our Record: Wins: ___ Losses: ___ Draws: ___
Minutes Played: _____

- My strengths as a player in today's match:

- My weaknesses as a player in today's match:

- Team strengths in today's match:

- Team weaknesses in today's match:

- Opponent's strengths:

- Opponent's weaknesses:

- What was the "difference" in today's match:

- What team adjustment would you suggest for the next match against this opponent?

- Who was the Player of the Match and why?

- Other comments (e.g., team strategy, attitude, preparation….)

Player Check-in

Above Average (+)   Average (O)   Below Average (–)

Health ___	*Nutrition:*	Grains ___
Sleep ___		Protein ___
Hydration ___		Veggies ___
Fitness ___		Fruit ___

Life Beyond Soccer ___

Quotable Quote:

____

____

Match Analysis I

Opponent: ___________ (W __ L __ D__) *Date:* ______ Result: ___
Pitch: ___________ Our Record: Wins: ___ Losses: ___ Draws: ___
Minutes Played: _____

- My strengths as a player in today's match:

- My weaknesses as a player in today's match:

- Team strengths in today's match:

- Team weaknesses in today's match:

- Opponent's strengths:

- Opponent's weaknesses:

- What was the "difference" in today's match:

- What team adjustment would you suggest for the next match against this opponent?

- Who was the Player of the Match and why?

- Other comments (e.g., team strategy, attitude, preparation....)

Player Check-in

Above Average (+)   Average (O)   Below Average (–)

Health ____	*Nutrition:*	Grains ____
Sleep ____		Protein ____
Hydration ____		Veggies ____
Fitness ____		Fruit ____

Life Beyond Soccer ____

Quotable Quote:

____

____

Match Analysis I

Opponent: ____________ (W __ L __ D__) *Date:* ______ Result: ___

Pitch: ___________Our Record: Wins: ___ Losses: ___ Draws: ___

Minutes Played: _____

- My strengths as a player in today's match:

- My weaknesses as a player in today's match:

- Team strengths in today's match:

- Team weaknesses in today's match:

- Opponent's strengths:

- Opponent's weaknesses:

- What was the "difference" in today's match:

- What team adjustment would you suggest for the next match against this opponent?

- Who was the Player of the Match and why?

- Other comments (e.g., team strategy, attitude, preparation....)

Player Check-in

Above Average (+)   Average (O)   Below Average (–)

Health ___	*Nutrition:*	Grains ___
Sleep ___		Protein ___
Hydration ___		Veggies ___
Fitness ___		Fruit ___

Life Beyond Soccer ___

Quotable Quote:

____

____

Match Analysis I

Opponent: ____________ (W __ L __ D__) *Date:* ______ Result: ___
Pitch: ___________Our Record: Wins: ___ Losses: ___ Draws: ___
Minutes Played: _____

- My strengths as a player in today's match:

- My weaknesses as a player in today's match:

- Team strengths in today's match:

- Team weaknesses in today's match:

- Opponent's strengths:

- Opponent's weaknesses:

___

- What was the "difference" in today's match:

- What team adjustment would you suggest for the next match against this opponent?

- Who was the Player of the Match and why?

- Other comments (e.g., team strategy, attitude, preparation....)

Player Check-in

Above Average (+)   Average (O)   Below Average (–)

Health	____	*Nutrition:* Grains	____
Sleep	____	Protein	____
Hydration	____	Veggies	____
Fitness	____	Fruit	____

Life Beyond Soccer ____

Quotable Quote:

____

____

Match Analysis I

Opponent: ____________ (W __ L __ D__) *Date:* ______ Result: ___
Pitch: ___________Our Record: Wins: ___ Losses: ___ Draws: ___
Minutes Played: _____

- My strengths as a player in today's match:

- My weaknesses as a player in today's match:

- Team strengths in today's match:

- Team weaknesses in today's match:

- Opponent's strengths:

- Opponent's weaknesses:

–   What was the "difference" in today's match:

–   What team adjustment would you suggest for the next match against this opponent?

–   Who was the Player of the Match and why?

–   Other comments (e.g., team strategy, attitude, preparation….)

Player Check-in

Above Average (+)   Average (O)   Below Average (–)

Health   ___   *Nutrition:*   Grains   ___
Sleep   ___   Protein   ___
Hydration ___   Veggies   ___
Fitness   ___   Fruit   ___

Life Beyond Soccer ___

Quotable Quote:

____

____

Match Analysis I

Opponent: _____________ (W __ L __ D__) *Date:* ______ Result: ___
Pitch: ____________Our Record: Wins: ___ Losses: ___ Draws: ___
Minutes Played: _____

- My strengths as a player in today's match:

- My weaknesses as a player in today's match:

- Team strengths in today's match:

- Team weaknesses in today's match:

- Opponent's strengths:

- Opponent's weaknesses:

– What was the "difference" in today's match:

– What team adjustment would you suggest for the next match against this opponent?

– Who was the Player of the Match and why?

– Other comments (e.g., team strategy, attitude, preparation….)

Player Check-in

Above Average (+)   Average (O)   Below Average (–)

Health	___	*Nutrition:*	Grains	___
Sleep	___		Protein	___
Hydration	___		Veggies	___
Fitness	___		Fruit	___

Life Beyond Soccer ___

Quotable Quote:

____

____

PERFORMANCE FEEDBACK

INSTRUCTIONS FOR PERFORMANCE FEEDBACK

At different times throughout your soccer season, camp, or tour, fill out one of the following Performance Feedback forms immediately after a match. This form helps you look closely at the stress you experience before and during a game. As an athlete, writing about stressors can help you manage those feelings in the future.

—MODEL—

Performance Feedback

Opponent: UNB   Date: September 18

What stressors did you experience before, during, and after this match?

Before the match I was concerned about the weather.

How did you experience this stress? Did it manifest in your thoughts, in the way you felt, or in the way you acted?

I worried that the weather would equalize play. We were definitely the better team and these thoughts made me———not nervous really, but a bit jittery.

Mark on this scale your level of excitement and motivation for the match.

0---5-/---10
      Too Low   Perfect   Too High

In a few words, describe your feelings at the various times in the day?

    Travel to match: *Excited*
    Warm up: *Pumped up*
    Just before the match: *Calm & focused*
    During the match: *It took me about 15 minutes to settle in.*
    After the match: *I felt like we earned the win.*

What techniques did you use to manage any stress you experienced? How effective were you in controlling this stress?

I talked to some of my teammates about the weather, not taking this team lightly, and how we needed to stay in control. I felt confident in my play and the team's once we kicked off. Talking to others helped me focus.

Describe how your stressors, excitement/motivation, and self-talk impacted your performance.

I think I was uneasy on the pitch for the first 15 minutes. Even before that, I wonder whether the way I talked to my teammates before the match may have made some of them nervous. I wanted to make them aware of the weather's influence… but maybe I just sounded nervous? Not sure. Otherwise, I felt ready for this match and settled in.

After unpacking your game-day mental state, what would you do differently to improve for the next match?

Maybe I sounded a bit hyper about the weather to my teammates. Again, not sure. I would think through my comments about the weather.

Additional Thoughts:
We won!

Performance Feedback

Opponent: _______________________ Date: _______________________

What stressors did you experience before, during and after this match?

How did you experience this stress? Did it manifest in your thoughts, in the way you felt, or in the way you acted?

Mark on this scale your level of excitement and motivation for the match.
0--5--10
      Too Low   Perfect   Too High

In a few words, describe your feelings at the various times in the day?

Travel to match:

Warm up:

Just before the match:

During the match:

After the match:

What techniques did you use to manage any stress you experienced? How effective were you in controlling this stress?

How was your self-talk? Positive, negative, thoughtful?

Describe how your stressors, excitement/motivation, and self-talk impacted your performance.

After unpacking your game-day mental state, what would you do differently to improve for the next match?

What's one thing you learned from completing this Performance Feedback form?

Performance Feedback

Opponent: _____________________ Date: _____________________

What stressors did you experience before, during and after this match?

How did you experience this stress? Did it manifest in your thoughts, in the way you felt, or in the way you acted?

Mark on this scale your level of excitement and motivation for the match.

0--5--10

    Too Low   Perfect   Too High

In a few words, describe your feelings at the various times in the day?

    Travel to match:

    Warm up:

    Just before the match:

    During the match:

    After the match:

What techniques did you use to manage any stress you experienced? How effective were you in controlling this stress?

How was your self-talk? Positive, negative, thoughtful?

Describe how your stressors, excitement/motivation, and self-talk impacted your performance.

After unpacking your game-day mental state, what would you do differently to improve for the next match?

What's one thing you learned from completing this Performance Feedback form?

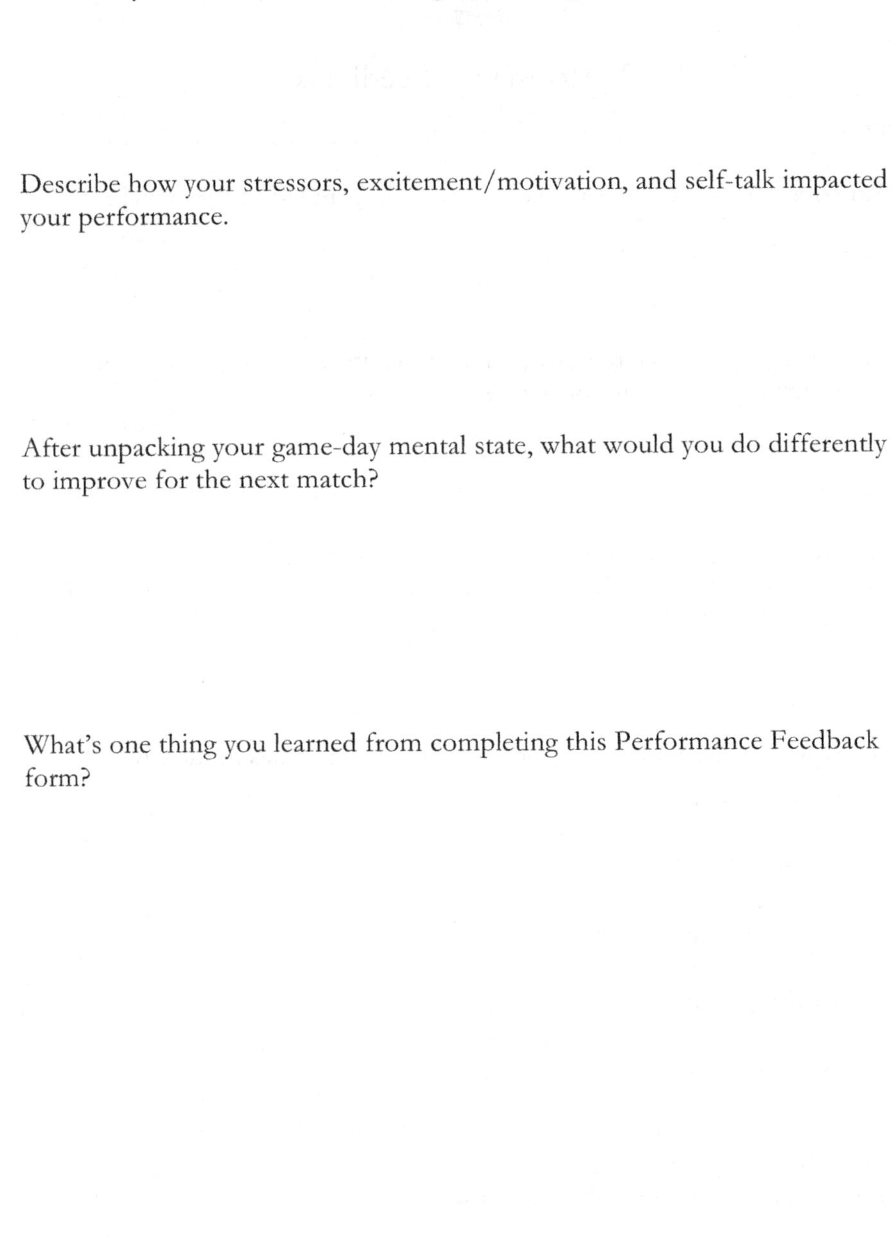

Performance Feedback

Opponent: _________________________ Date: _____________________

What stressors did you experience before, during and after this match?

How did you experience this stress? Did it manifest in your thoughts, in the way you felt, or in the way you acted?

Mark on this scale your level of excitement and motivation for the match.

0------------------------------------5------------------------------------10
    Too Low   Perfect   Too High

In a few words, describe your feelings at the various times in the day?

    Travel to match:

    Warm up:

    Just before the match:

    During the match:

    After the match:

What techniques did you use to manage any stress you experienced? How effective were you in controlling this stress?

How was your self-talk? Positive, negative, thoughtful?

Describe how your stressors, excitement/motivation, and self-talk impacted your performance.

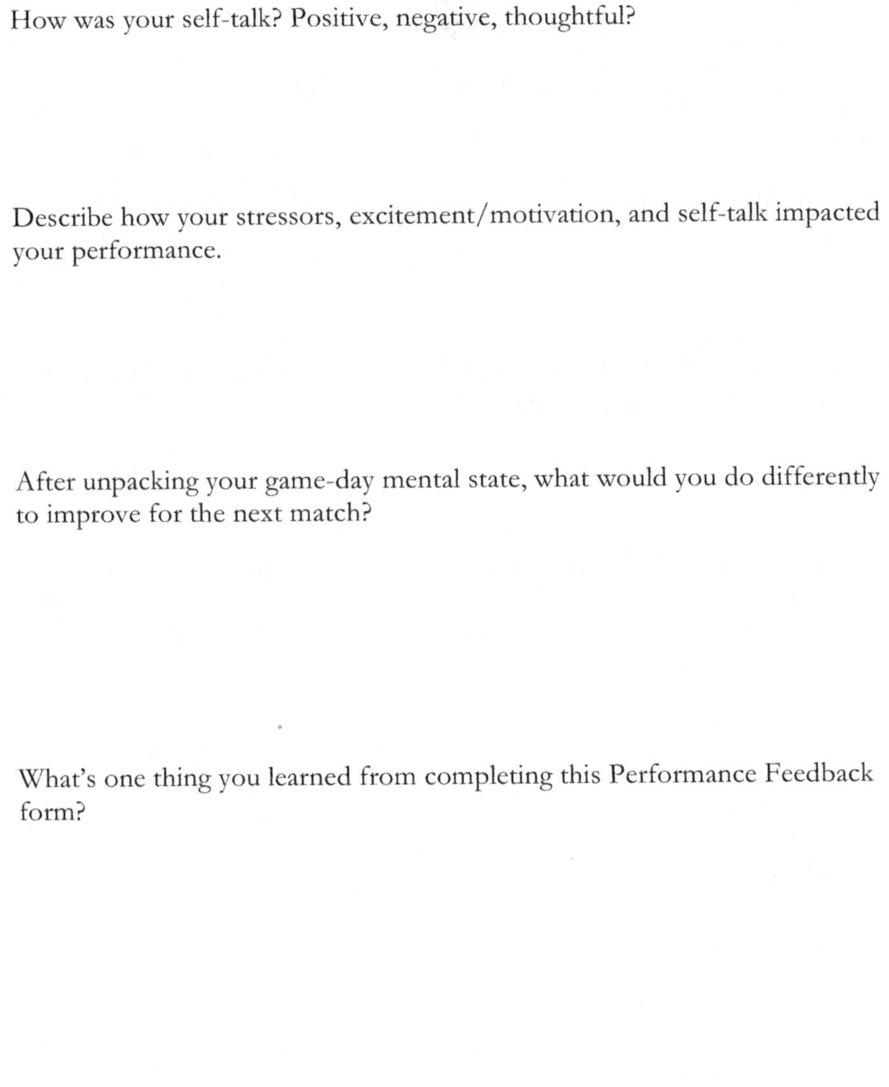

After unpacking your game-day mental state, what would you do differently to improve for the next match?

What's one thing you learned from completing this Performance Feedback form?

Performance Feedback

Opponent: _____________________ Date: _____________________

What stressors did you experience before, during and after this match?

How did you experience this stress? Did it manifest in your thoughts, in the way you felt, or in the way you acted?

Mark on this scale your level of excitement and motivation for the match.

0--5--10

      Too Low   Perfect   Too High

In a few words, describe your feelings at the various times in the day?

    Travel to match:

    Warm up:

    Just before the match:

    During the match:

    After the match:

What techniques did you use to manage any stress you experienced? How effective were you in controlling this stress?

How was your self-talk? Positive, negative, thoughtful?

Describe how your stressors, excitement/motivation, and self-talk impacted your performance.

After unpacking your game-day mental state, what would you do differently to improve for the next match?

What's one thing you learned from completing this Performance Feedback form?

Performance Feedback

Opponent: _____________________ Date: _____________________

What stressors did you experience before, during and after this match?

How did you experience this stress? Did it manifest in your thoughts, in the way you felt, or in the way you acted?

Mark on this scale your level of excitement and motivation for the match.

0---5---10

      Too Low   Perfect   Too High

In a few words, describe your feelings at the various times in the day?

    Travel to match:

    Warm up:

    Just before the match:

    During the match:

    After the match:

What techniques did you use to manage any stress you experienced? How effective were you in controlling this stress?

How was your self-talk? Positive, negative, thoughtful?

Describe how your stressors, excitement/motivation, and self-talk impacted your performance.

After unpacking your game-day mental state, what would you do differently to improve for the next match?

What's one thing you learned from completing this Performance Feedback form?

MATCH ANALYSIS II

INSTRUCTIONS FOR MATCH ANALYSIS II

Throughout your soccer camp or season, you'll have opportunities to analyze matches that you've watched in person, on TV, or online. Filling out the Match Analysis II can help you look more objectively at those games. The *MAII* is a learning activity that will challenge you to watch a match more critically, more fully, and more like a coach than an athlete. Unpacking a soccer match with the Match Analysis II will guide you to becoming a more thoughtful student of the game.

Review the model Match Analysis II on the following couple of pages.

—MODEL—

Match Analysis II

Team #1 Torrence HS

Wins: *6* Losses: *4* Draws: *2*
Date: *September 29*

Alignment of Players:
4-4-2

Strengths:
*Outside midfielders
made great runs.*

Weaknesses:
*They seemed to relax
when they were up 2-0.
Young.*

Team #2 Freedom HS

Wins: *7* Losses: *3* Draws: *1*
Pitch: *Hosmer*

Alignment of Players:
1st half 4-4-2   2nd: 4-3-3

Strengths:
*Sweeper
Center Mid*

Weaknesses:
*Didn't use space well.
Their coach: a screamer.*

Half-time adjustments & effects:

*None. They came
out flat. Over confident.*

*Went to a 4-3-3 for more
targets up front. Created
more opportunities.*

General Comments:

Forwards
Fast

Midfielders
Athletic

Defenders
Moved well together.

Keeper
*Confident—great technique—
Team leader*

Forwards
Lacked movement

Midfielders
*Lost composure—
their talk was not
constructive.*

Defenders
Seemed spacey.

Keeper
*Poor positioning.
No talk after 2nd goal*

Player of the Match:

#6—left mid. His runs through the D opened up huge space. He always encouraged his mates. He's the kind of player I'd like to be. Great goal.

Sweeper—he kept his cool. It's not easy leading young players.

Moment of the Match:

#6's run through the D and his one-touch to the near post. Sweet String Music! Magic!

Final Analysis:

THS needed to work on the simple things: move to space and play the way you face. They were a lot younger than FHS and just needed to try to play within themselves. It's like you told us over the last two years. Play the fundamentals—it's a simple game so keep it that way. As for FHS, they didn't stay focused for the whole match. Their coach needed to teach not yell—the guy embarrassed himself.

Match Analysis II

Team #1_____________________ v. Team #2_____________________

Wins: __ Losses: __ Draws: __   Wins: __ Losses: __ Draws: __

Date: ____________________   Pitch: ____________________

Alignment of Players: Alignment of Players:

Strengths: Strengths:

Weaknesses: Weaknesses:

Half-time adjustments   Half-time adjustments
& effects: & effects:

General Comments:

Forwards   Forwards

Midfielders   Midfielders

Defenders   Defenders

Keeper   Keeper

Players of the Match:

Moment of the Match:

Final Analysis:

General Comments:

Match Analysis II

Team #1_____________________ v. Team #2_____________________

Wins: __ Losses: __ Draws: __   Wins: __ Losses: __ Draws: __

Date: _____________________   Pitch: _____________________

Alignment of Players: Alignment of Players:

Strengths: Strengths:

Weaknesses: Weaknesses:

Half-time adjustments   Half-time adjustments
& effects: & effects:

General Comments:

Forwards   Forwards

Midfielders   Midfielders

Defenders   Defenders

Keeper   Keeper

Players of the Match:

Moment of the Match:

Final Analysis:

General Comments:

Match Analysis II

Team #1_____________________ v. Team #2_____________________

Wins: __ Losses: __ Draws: __   Wins: __ Losses: __ Draws: __

Date: _____________________   Pitch: _____________________

Alignment of Players: Alignment of Players:

Strengths: Strengths:

Weaknesses: Weaknesses:

Half-time adjustments   Half-time adjustments
& effects: & effects:

General Comments:

Forwards   Forwards

Midfielders   Midfielders

Defenders   Defenders

Keeper   Keeper

Players of the Match:

Moment of the Match:

Final Analysis:

General Comments:

NOTES PAGE

Date_______________   Title_______________

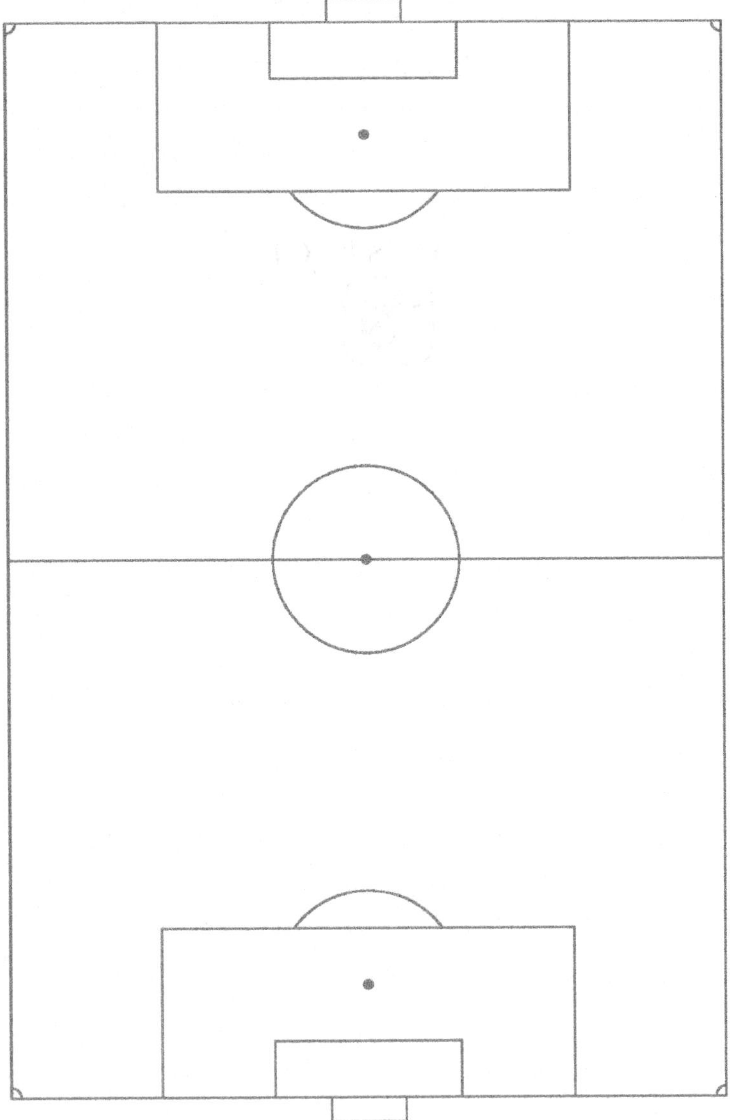

Date________________   Title______________

Notes

Date________________   Title________________

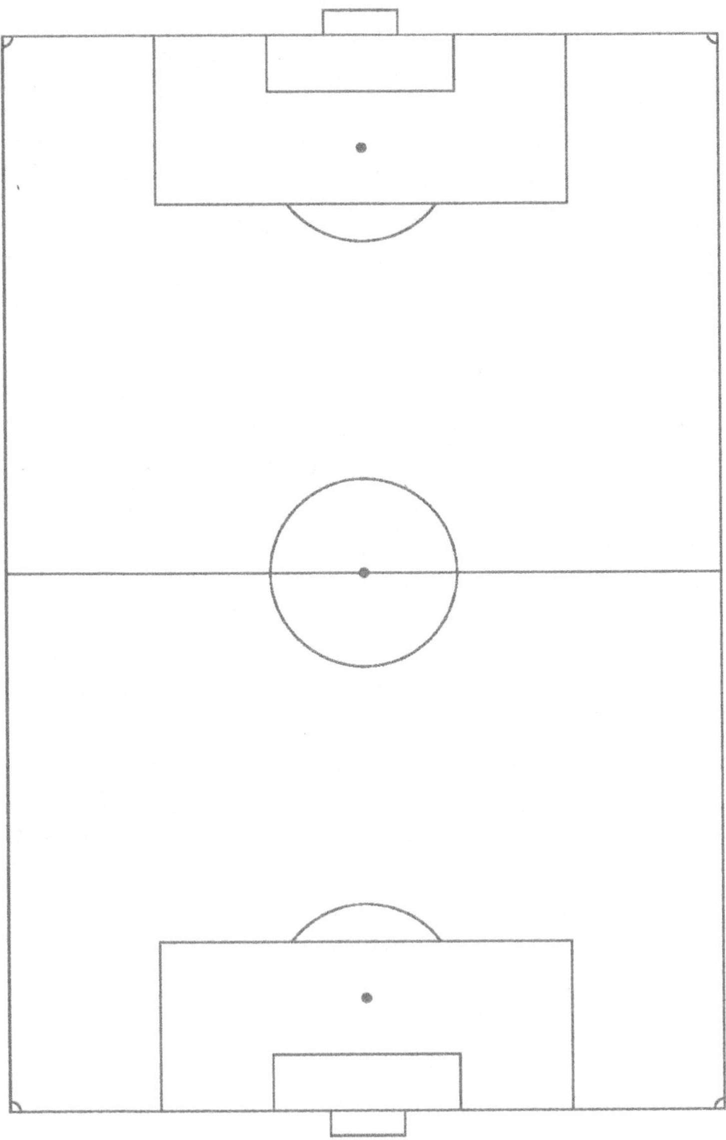

Date________________   Title________________

Notes

131

Date_____________   Title_____________

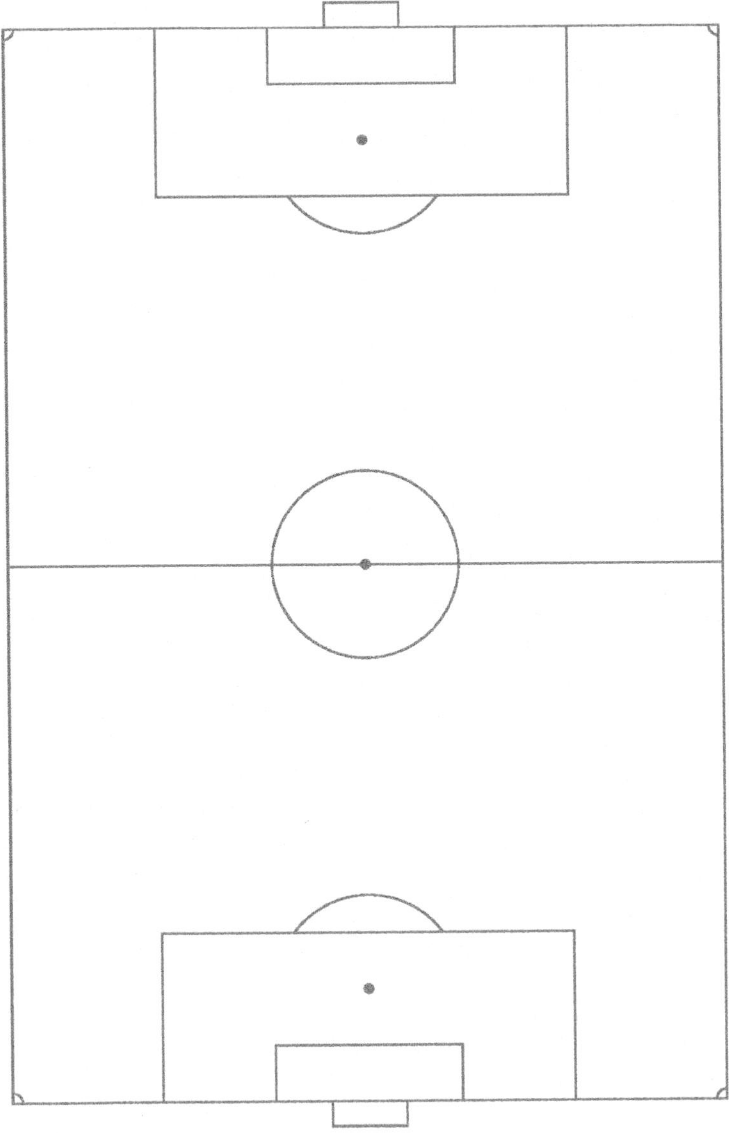

Date________________   Title________________

Notes

133

Date_______________   Title______________

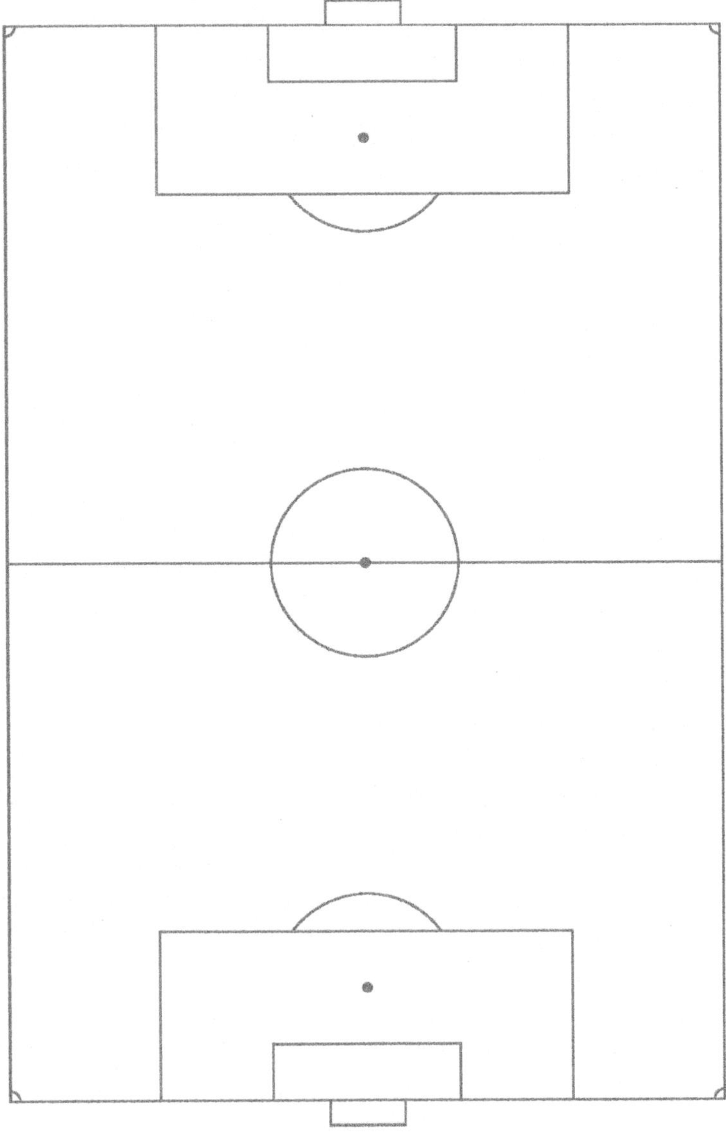

Date_______________   Title_______________

Notes

_____

Date_____________   Title_____________

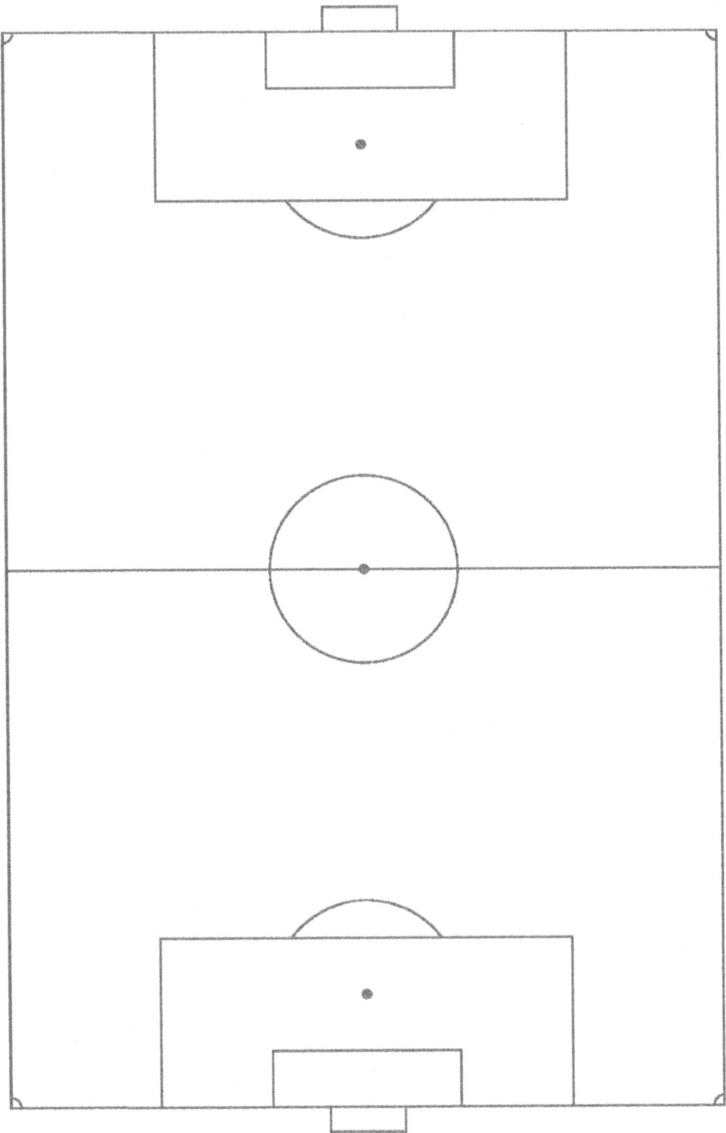

Date_______________   Title_______________

Notes

ABOUT THE AUTHORS

Richard Kent

Amy Edwards

Richard Kent is a professor at the University of Maine. A former Olympic Development Program coach, Kent took 30 state of Maine teams to England in the 1980s and 1990s. The author of many books, including *Writing on the Bus*, *The Athlete's Workbook*, and *Soccer Team Notebook* with Amy Edwards, Kent works with teams, athletes, and coaches across the USA.

Amy Edwards is the Head Women's Soccer Coach at Gonzaga University and has been a collegiate coach since 1993. She started her coaching career working in youth clubs and continued in the Olympic Development Programs of Oklahoma and Missouri. Coach Edwards holds national coaching licenses from both USSF and NSCAA.

For more information on athletes' journals and team notebooks, check out this resource website:

WritingAthletes.com

141

Write. Learn. Perform.

Made in the USA
Monee, IL
07 July 2026

56551146R00079